Marked for Ministry

By:

Dawnn M. Burrell

Published by
Dawnn M. Burrell
Grand Rapids, Michigan

Scriptures
All Scripture quotations used in this book are from the Holy Bible, New King James Version®. Copyright © 1982 by Thomas Nelson, Inc.
Used by permission.

Definitions
Dictionary.com and Merriam-Webster Dictionary Online

Edited by
James Mack, CPI

Book Cover Design by
4UGRAPHICS - Tasha Murray
Used by permission

Photos by
JC Penney Portrait Studios
Used by permission

ISBN 9780615301747

Acknowledgements

To God, who gave me the desire, knowledge, wisdom and understanding to complete this project of His and I'm glad He entrusted me to do it.

To my husband Fred, who encouraged me to fulfill every area of ministry that God has given me.

To Rose Oliver, who encouraged me by saying "go head now, you go girl."

To James Mack, my cousin, who shared with me his experiences and pointers in writing his first book. Who also encouraged me to write and for taking time out of his busy schedule to edit this book.

To Nicki Tardy, who prayed for me and stood in the gap for me while I finished this project.

To Tasha Murray, my cousin of 4UGraphics, for her artwork in designing the cover and the layout of this book.

To Rose Hammond, for encouraging me to bring this book to pass and sharing with me her experiences on writing her book.

To all of you I say, thank you for believing this book would come to pass. May God bless you like only He can.

Introduction

This book was written because some things that we have gone through in life have marked us for ministry. Some times we as God's children don't understand why we go through different things and why different things happen to us. Instead of saying "why me" we should be thanking God for creating us and using us. It is truly an honor and a privilege to be used by God. Too many times we look at what has happened to us as being negative when in fact, it's really positive. For it says in Romans 8:28 "And we know that all things work together for good to those who love God, to those who are the called according to His purpose." When you look at what happens in your life according to Romans 8:28 that's something to shout about!

Let's look at the definition of "marked" according to Merriam-Webster Dictionary Online, "having an identifying mark." We have visible and invisible marks. God uses both marks to develop ministry in our lives. It's because the invisible marks of a person house; pain, hurt, bitterness, sickness, frustration, low self-esteem, pride and so much more. The *visible marks of a person are the result of the invisible marks.*

When we talk about dealing with the visible and invisible marks it is the invisible marks that we don't want to deal with or don't know how to deal with. We really need to be honest with ourselves about our marks. I know for some that's hard to do, but I have found when I'm honest about whom the real Dawnn is, I can look at myself in the mirror and then go to God for Him to fix what's wrong.

When we have visible and invisible marks we need to remember they do leave impressions. We have to decide what type of impressions we want the marks to leave. I don't know about you, but I want to leave impressions that will not only help me, but they can help someone else.

I pray that as you read this book that you would let the Holy Spirit minister healing, deliverance and strength to you. I pray that as you read this book that you would become encouraged to finish your race.

Table of Contents

Chapter 1:   "Purpose"   Page 1

Chapter 2:   "Gifts"   Page 17

Chapter 3:   "Family"   Page 31

Chapter 4:   "Marriage"   Page 45

Chapter 5:   "God's Mark"   Page 61

Chapter 1

Purpose

Before we talk about being marked for ministry we are going to talk about in this chapter "Purpose". I believe that we not only get marked because we are God's children, but also because of God's purpose for our lives. In Chapter 2 we are going to talk about some of the gifts of God, because you can't talk about being marked for ministry until you talk about purpose and gifts.

The definition of purpose that I like according to Merriam-Webster Online Dictionary is, "something set up as an object or end to be attained." When God gave us a purpose He knew that we could attain it as long as He was the One guiding us through the process.

When the Lord told me to write this book I was very excited. I began to prepare myself by going out and buying notebooks and pens. I outlined the book. I had attended a renowned conference and when I got there they had different workshops and one of the workshops was on writing a book. When I attended the workshop and listened to what the speaker was saying I knew then that I was suppose to write a book. Why? Because the speaker was saying what you need to do to get started and how you know when there is a book(s) inside of you. Well all the things the speaker had spoken I had already done. However, the speaker said you have to keep at it and you may not get the words to say when you think you will.

When I returned home from the conference I picked up the book again, but I lost interest and it seemed like there wasn't enough in me to put in a book. Even though, I remembered what was said in the workshop, I still put the book down.

Well this book would keep coming up in my spirit and I said I'm going to finish it. Well years went by and one day God let me know this was one thing that He had purposed for me to do. At the same time I felt this was the last chance He was giving me to complete it. I also came to realize that the Holy Ghost is in me and He was the One that was going to speak through me and not me.

When God has called us to do something there are times when it can seem impossible and very difficult to accomplish. There are times when the devil will bring things your way to discourage you. There are times when life itself will bring things to you that you give in to and you get off track. When these things happen this is when we have to press through the mess, the distractions and the deceptions.

Thanks be unto God, who gives us grace along with His anointing to complete what we are purposed to do. Whatever God has called you to do make sure you do it in the grace and anointing that is there for you, because without them the project won't do what it was intended to do.

Our purpose has an audience. Yes, there are people that need what you have. Just like we say sometimes God send me some help, there are people that are saying the same thing and we have to get ready to be their help because they are waiting for us.

I have had some bumpy, smooth and crooked roads that I have traveled to bring me where I am today and I'm thankful that God's grace and anointing didn't run out on me.

I'm not saying it's smooth sailing from here. I am saying up to this point in my life the road has not always been smooth. One thing we can be sure of, that is as long as we are alive God is not done with us. There are going to be all kinds of things that happen in our life. There are going to be some things that come in our life to make us and try to break us. There are going to be some things that come in our life to cause us to quit and give up on God.

One thing about purpose from God, it will lead you in the right direction and God will be glorified. God wants the glory out of our life. Lets look at Job 1:8, God said to satan "have you considered My servant Job...".

When I think about this it reminds me that God is in control. Even though God said to satan "have you....", God wasn't asking satan a question that He didn't know the answer to. Not only did God know the answer, but also He knew everything that was going to result from it, a victorious outcome.

When we read the Book of Job, our conclusion has to be that what Job went through was his purpose in life.

Job's purpose in life wasn't to become the greatest or wealthiest person in the East. Job's purpose was to be blameless, upright, fear God, shun evil and to keep his family covered. Yes, Job had sheep, camels, oxen, donkeys and staff, but they weren't his purpose to obtain. These were the blessings from God for him obeying God.

God made Job the greatest and wealthiest person in the East because Job put God first and worked at fulfilling his purpose. The emphasis in the Word wasn't Job's possessions, but his purpose.

In the beginning things for Job were going well, then well turned to worst when he lost his possessions, children, body affected, wife saying the wrong things and his friends not understanding what was happening to him. If Job had closed the communication line to God, Job would not have had a ending that was far greater than his beginning.

As we travel through life we must keep the communication open between God and us. We must not allow our situations and circumstances to change our communication with God. The worst thing that we can do is not talk to God. For it is in the difficult times of our lives that God is a very present help.

Every one of us has purpose inside of us. No matter how much or how little you have, God is requiring it of His children to produce the fruit.

We are living in the last days and we are in the last hour. The clock is ticking and every second and minute is very important. Instead of us taking an inventory of what we have, we need to take an inventory of what we have and have not completed or, even started.

If you don't know what your purpose is, don't be ashamed. There are a lot of Christians who don't know their purpose. There are some Christians that think they're living out their purpose, but they are not. Some Christians are living out purposes that others told them what their purpose was, without seeking God for themselves.

Don't look at your age. Before you were conceived in your mother's womb, you had purpose. Jeremiah was a young boy when God revealed to him what his purpose was.

When God told Jeremiah what He wanted him to do Jeremiah became fearful. There are some people that God has told what He has called them to do and they won't accept the call or some try and get out of it. Look at Jeremiah, he was a young boy and God was calling him to speak to the nations ~ to adults, what a call. God is so good that He didn't change His plans for Jeremiah, He tells Jeremiah; "Before I formed you in the womb

I knew you; Before you were born I sanctified you; And I ordained you a prophet to the nations." Jeremiah 1:5

God goes from telling Jeremiah what He has called him to do, to teach Jeremiah what he has called him to do by saying "Jeremiah what do you see?" Jeremiah 1:11 Jeremiah stepped up to the call ~ to his purpose. We have to let the ultimate Teacher ~ teach us how to fulfill our purpose.

When God revealed to you what your purpose was did you give Him excuses? When God reveals to us what our purpose is, He is not looking for excuses, doubts, fears, woe is me mentality, etc. God is looking for us to stand up to the call and to embrace it. God is looking for us to be excited that He has chose us out of so many others to do only what we can do. Every person is special to God. Every person has a part in God's will. Before we were placed in our mother's womb we were called by God.

When I looked back over my life, especially when I was a child, I knew there was something different about me. I noticed there were times when I would say something, do something or act differently, but I didn't really realize it until after I did it. I began to pay a little more attention to myself, but then I made up my mind that, it was just a coincidence. There were times when I would prophesy, but I didn't know I was prophesying I was told; oh that's your sixth sense.

Now if I were brought up in a house where we were taught about the spiritual gifts I wouldn't been led to believe I had a sixth sense, but rather I had the gift of prophecy.

Just like Jeremiah when we find out that God will be with us as we fulfill our purpose we will do it with all boldness and in love. When we come to know our purpose we can't be moved by what people will say to us or how they will react to us. I truly believe that God will see us all through everything that He has called us to. I believe that God will be there to teach us how to fulfill the purpose that He has so designed for us.

When God reveals to us what our purpose is our age won't matter to Him. God doesn't live in a box and He doesn't flow according to our comfort zones and what we think is possible.

We are living in a time where we need to do quickly what God has called us to do. No matter how far fetched it may seem or how impossible it may seem. God's Word says; "For with God nothing will be impossible." Luke 1:37 (NKJV)

We have to remember everyday that we serve the Only true wise and living God. We serve the God that there is nothing too hard for Him to do. As a matter of fact, God is the Creator of all things. God even created our purpose. I believe we sometimes forget that. When God created us He knew what we could and could not do. What is most important is God knows what He can do and we need to believe that God can do the impossible.

As we have come to know everybody was born with a purpose. Some people found out early in life what it was. Some found out later in life and there are some that haven't found out yet. Whether if we found out early or later in life we found out.

For those of you that know what your purpose is, you must take ownership of it and bring it to its fulfillment. For those of you that don't know what your purpose is be still as you seek God for His answer. What I mean by be still ~ don't be doing a lot of stuff where you can't hear the Holy Ghost speak to you. If there are things in your life that you need to get rid of, then get rid of them quickly, so the Holy Ghost can speak to you and God can use you.

I want to speak to the parents. If you have not sought God about your child's purpose, I encourage you to do so. It is our responsibility as parents to find out what our children have been created to do. If you need help with this then, seek wise counsel. As you noticed I said seek wise counsel. This simply means Christian counseling. For in Psalm 1:1 it says, "Blessed is the man Who walks not in the counsel of the ungodly." (NKJV) You don't want the world's opinion to influence you and your child's life. For those that are going to be parents my advice to you is the same.

A lot of what's happening in the world with some children is the parent's fault. We as parents in raising some of our children, we have left God out. God has to be in every part of the raising, not only in the part where we are trying to justify what we are saying to them. To those that have allowed God to direct you in raising your child and they're doing things contrary to God's Will for their life, just hold on because a change is coming.

Make no mistake about it; when God reveals to us our purpose and our children's purpose, He knows what He's talking about. Remember God knows everything about us our beginning and end all at the same time. Psalm 100:3 says; "Know that the LORD, He is God; It is He who made us; and not we ourselves; We are His people and the sheep of His pasture."

When God reveals our purpose to us we must not think more highly of ourselves and become prideful. We must step up to the batter's plate and hit a home run. We can't come up with excuses as to why we can't fulfill our purpose.

Every purpose in all of us is very important and unique. God's ultimate purpose is kingdom building and our purpose was meant to connect with God's purpose for the fulfillments. Remember no can fulfill your purpose, except you.

Another thing we need to look at concerning purpose is; why am I still alive? Some of you are like me. Your past wasn't clean. God saved you from drugs, alcohol, fornication and the list goes on and on.

I remember asking God, why am I still alive and my best friend was murdered when she was 21 years old? Why am I still alive when friends died of AIDS, friends on drugs, alcohol and some went to prison? God began to unfold to me my purpose. What He told Jeremiah in Jeremiah 1:5, 9, 10; what Paul told Timothy in First Timothy 4:11-16, Second Timothy 4:1-5 and what Jesus told His disciples, in Acts 1:8, He told me.

Just because I'm still alive and living out my purpose

doesn't mean I was any better than my friends who died, strung out on drugs and alcohol and went to prison. I had my own issues too, it was God's decision to bring me where I am now.

When God reveals to us what our purpose is we need to get excited to the degree that God chose us and He wants to use us for His glory. What an honor and a privilege that the Almighty God the Creator of the world chose us.

Chapter 2

Gifts

Every person that God created has a gift or gifts inside of them to be used for God's glory. In order to know what the gift is, you need to seek God. Sometimes God speaks to you and tells you your gift without seeking Him.

When some people seek God about what He has gifted them with, some are fine with the gift, some are disappointed with the gifts and some say I rebuke you satan you're a liar. Those that are disappointed and rebuke satan are one in the same, because they don't understand the full function of the gift working through them and how important they are in the Body of Jesus Christ with their gift.

It is one thing to be disappointed when finding out what our gift is, but it is another thing to think satan is talking to you when in fact it is God. I believe that when we go to God about our gift we need to go to Him with a clear mind. What I mean by this is, not seeking God with the gift you want already in your mind. When God reveals your gift to you, you won't be disappointed and make the mistake of who is talking to you.

Remember every gift of God is precious, valuable and needed. When people are given gifts, God is saying I have entrusted to your care something that is so powerful. Why are His gifts powerful? Because His gifts were created to win souls back to Him, to encourage the bow down head (down trodden), to set the captives free from bondage, to heal, to bring people out of poverty, to restore families and the list goes on.

Some people want the gift of pastor, teacher, evangelist, prophet, and apostle because these gifts are more out front. The truth of the matter is to be on the frontline you have to have special training, past the most difficult test, stay awake and study when others are sleeping and stay at home when others go out. You have to be occupied with special armour and know how to put it on and know how to use the right weapons when the situation arises. Even though sometimes these gifts look easy when they're in operation, they are not. The preparation it takes to be used by God is sometimes challenging, difficult and misunderstood.

When God gifted us He knew just what He was doing. You see along with the gifts they are personalized according to our character. That's why when you see a person flowing in their gift it seems so natural to see them flow in that gift. This is why I believe we were operating in some aspects of our gifts when we were not saved. As I mentioned in Chapter One I knew things and had wisdom about different things, but I didn't know God, so I just thought I had an insight about a situation (a sixth sense).

When I look back I sometimes say I wish my parents and myself would of known God then, so I could have been completely flowing in my gifts from my youth. As you see I said "known God." The truth is we knew of Him, but there was no personal relationship with Him. At the same time, I'm grateful to God that I'm still alive, I'm saved, I have a personal relationship with Him, I know what my gifts are and I'm flowing in them.

"Different Gifts Same Spirit"

When we read in Romans 12:4-8, Ephesians 4:10-11 and First Corinthians 12:1-11 we see God's gifts outlined. There are different gifts, but the same Spirit. God is a diverse God and that is because He is a limitless God. In other words, the functioning of God's gifts has no limits because the Holy Spirit is so powerful that He causes all the gifts to function at the same time and you can't put the Holy Spirit in a box.

Can you imagine everybody having the same gift, everybody doing the same thing, we would be like robots. The gift that you have is designed to minister to certain people. Whether you're planting the seed or watering the seed be effective. Whether if you are doing things in ministry or on your job you want your work to be fruitful. It doesn't matter if you are planting or watering the seed. What matters, is you are still alive to be used by God to plant or water the seed.

"Being Content"

We have to learn to be content in the gift that God has given us. We need to be fine with the gift, accept the gift and really count it an honor and a privilege that God created us with a gift to be used for His glory. God didn't make any mistakes when He placed the gift inside of us. If we don't produce the fruit from our gift, then it's our fault.

When you look at one definition of content it means, "being satisfied with what one is or has, not wanting more or anything else." (Dictionary.com). So many times we limit ourselves to this definition. This definition is fine, but there's another definition of content that I like to share with you that the Holy Ghost gave me some years ago it simply means be content of who you are, where you are and what you have, but be ready to move to the next level or place in God."

Yes, there are areas in our life that might not change and that's okay. What's not okay is when we are content with who we are and where we are, knowing that we are not supposed to stay there forever and we don't do what we're suppose to do to change. Being content and confident work hand in hand, because when you're content, confidence is produced.

"Being Confident"

One definition of confident is, "having strong belief or full assurance." (Dictionary.com) When you are confident about yourself or anything, you have an assurance that causes your self-esteem to be high instead of low. When we have a high self-esteem we have to be careful that we don't turn our confidence into arrogance. Make sure you know the difference between being confident and being arrogant. When you are confident you feel you can take on the world. When you are confident in your gift you won't be moved by others that are operating in their gift. When you are confident in your gift you don't operate outside of your gift. When you are confident about your gift you recognize that your gift is to help and not hinder.

When you are confident in your gift you know that when you are operating in it you will produce fruit. When you are confident in your gift you are secure in the Holy Ghost. All of these reasons of being confident in your gift are really important, because to follow God you can't be unsure and of who you are.

When you are confident in your gift you will walk in victory. Being victorious sums up what being confident in our gift is.

"No Competing"

When we look at the gift that is inside of us and the gift inside of others we must be very careful not to become competitive. God's gifts are spiritual and not carnal. One thing is sure, that is the Holy Ghost does not compete against Himself. Let me say that again, the Holy Ghost does not compete against Himself. I have seen people do this and it tells me that they are not secure about the gift they have and they don't really know the Holy Ghost like they say they do and they don't really know themselves. I know some people will get mad at me about this statement that I just made. I didn't say it to make anyone mad, but rather for some to examine themselves and the truth about the Holy Ghost, so God can really use them to their highest potential.

I believe the devil wants the saints to become competitive to get us off focus and to let our guards down. The gifts were given to work hand in hand. That's why in Ephesians 4:12 it says; "For the equipping of the saints for the work of ministry, for the edifying of the Body of Christ."

I am satisfied with the gifts that God put in me and I don't desire any others and that's the way we all are suppose to be. When God revealed to me my gifts my soul leaped with joy. Not because these gifts are apart of the fivefold gifts, but rather He cared enough about me, to save me, and gifted me to do His work.

Don't ever let anyone down play what God has given you. If you are a preacher, usher, missionary, singer, helper or admin- istrator know that you are needed in the Body of Jesus Christ and the Body of Jesus Christ doesn't function like it should when you are missing. Don't get caught up in competition, but rather let God's light shine in you and through you, so He can be gloried. Competition is a weapon of the devil to distract you, to deceive you and to steer you away from God.

"Responsibilities of the Gift"

There are some Christians who are content with just coming to service after service because they don't want the complete package of being saved. In the package of being saved along with your spiritual gifts are the responsibilities that go with the gifts. The responsibilities of our gift are to take care of it. We are to always protect our gift. We are not to abuse our gift and neither are we suppose to let others abuse our gift. We are responsible to value our gifts. We are responsible to bringing our gift to maturity. We are not to prostitute our gifts ~ yes I said it because it is happening more and more.

We are not to run from our gift because of the responsibilities. You can run all you want to; the gifts are still in you. Are you running from the responsibilities of the gift that God has entrusted to you? If you are, please stop running and ask God for forgiveness, repent and enjoy the finer things in life. A life of abundance! Everything that God gives us, He wants us to take care of it because it belongs to Him. Just like us, if we let someone borrow something of ours we expect it to be returned to us in good condition like we gave it. Let's face it, when we loan something to someone we expect them to be responsible with our possessions. In other words, we want them to take care of what we have entrusted them with. God is no different!

Some saints don't want to use their gifts because other saints have used and abused them. I have heard saints say; they're tired of working in the ministry. When you ask them why they will tell you how badly they were treated; they didn't even get a simple thank you.

You know it is not hard to tell someone thank you and to

treat someone nice it doesn't cost you anything, but it will return a reward to you from God.

"Operating in the wrong Gift"

I have seen people operating in the wrong gift. When this happens the ministry is not flowing like it should and neither is it growing to its capacity because someone is out of order. When we become apart of a ministry it is very important that we are called to that ministry. I am talking about being called to a local Church and working in that local Church's ministry. We have to stop ministry hopping. It's time out for people being able to go serve on this ministry and that ministry for the wrong reasons. I'd rather see you sit down and hear from God and then go where He tells you to serve.

When you are operating in the wrong gift you can hurt yourself and others. You might not be doing it intentionally, but it happens. When you are operating in the wrong gift you have wasted a lot of time. Also what you have done is stunted your growth in that gift. When some people are in leadership positions and they are not leaders, they can lead the people in the ditch. I just believe when your gift is flowing in the Body of Jesus Christ correctly, it will produce fruit.

When a person is operating in the right gift, it is so productive for the Body of Jesus Christ. The harvest will be; seeing people's spirit lifted, people encouraged, people walking in victory, people delivered, people saved, marriages restored, families reconciled and the results will continue to manifest. The love and joy of God will flow out of you and your reward will be great.

Chapter 3

Family

This chapter is on the family and when you talk about family you may or may not offend someone. This chapter was not written to offend my family. When God gave me the title of this book He didn't tell me that there was going to be a chapter on family. When I began to write God began to unfold things about my past that I didn't have a clue that He wanted told.

God literally ministered to me and kept saying to me; "you are marked for ministry. I'm going to take your marks and heal people." So, as you read on and if anything you can relate to or you are dealing with stop and allow the Holy Spirit to fix and heal you. I pray that you would finish this book and tell someone else you know to read this book, that can benefit from the healing that is in this book.

I don't know about you, but when I think about family I think about strength, unity, love, peace and trust. The families that have these characteristics were taught these things early in life and they taught them to the next generation. If you talk to someone in that family, they will tell you who taught them and who taught that person.

As for me when I was growing up my mother and grand-mother, (mostly my grandmother) raised me. I am the youngest of four and there were and still are times where being the baby is a benefit and not a benefit.

When I was 1 ½ years old my father died at the age of 30. Even though being that young you would think I didn't get an opportunity to know him, but on the contrary I did. I remember there were times that I would wake up in the middle of the night as an adolescence and my pillow would be soaked and wet from me crying. When I would awake I felt this void within me and I would say; I miss my father.

As I began to get older the wet pillow didn't stop. I would

go on day after day with a void in my life that couldn't be filled. One day I asked my mother about my father and our relationship and her answer unfolded the answer to my tears.

My mother told me that my father's relationship with me was different than my sisters and brother. My mother told me my father did things with me and for me that he didn't do with and for my siblings and he spent more time with me then he did with them. As I grew up and knowing how much time my father spent with me, the things he did with me, the void was still there.

Parents and future parents deposit good things in your child, do all that God tells you to do because it will make a difference in their life and your life. I am 52 years old and all the time my father had with me was 1 ½ years. In that time he left a lasting impression in my life.

The void in my life was really a mark for ministry. When I was growing up I didn't get along to well with my siblings. Even some adults I didn't get along with.

There were things in my life that I felt like Joseph when he told his brothers about his dreams Genesis 37:5~8. Joseph had dreamed some dreams and to him they were good dreams. They were exciting dreams. They were dreams that he wanted to share with his brothers. Even though when his brothers heard the first dream it caused them to hate him, that wasn't Joseph's intent.

Joseph dreamed the second dream and shared it with his brothers, but this time their hatred for him grew worst. Even though Joseph was Jacob's favorite son Joseph still felt like an outsider by his brothers. By Joseph sharing with his brothers about the dreams he had to feel that it was going to bring them closer. He had to feel, maybe if I tell them my dreams they would like me and accept me. I believe this is what Joseph was after, to be close and accepted by his brothers.

It wasn't Joseph's fault that his brothers hated him; it was his father's fault. It was Jacob that showed partiality toward Joseph. In Genesis 37:2 Jacob put Joseph in charge over his brothers. This why in the latter part of Genesis 37:2 it says, "Joseph brought a bad report of them to his father." In Genesis 37:14 confirms Jacob putting Joseph over his brothers because Jacob wanted to know what and how they were doing with Jacob's possessions.

Most babies in a family get special attention. Not only do they get special attention, but they get special privileges, extra things, they tend to get away with more because they are the baby. Like Joseph, with me it really wasn't anything that I did that caused me sometimes not to get along well with my siblings, it was because how others treated me because of me being the baby.

Joseph was just being himself walking in the authority his father gave him and to top it off his father gave him a tunic of many colors. When his father gave him the tunic of many colors it marked Joseph for ministry and for his entitlement to the inheritance. When I received special attention, special privileges, extra things, I became marked for ministry. I also remember my mother bought me two coats on two different occasions that were of many colors. I didn't think and I still don't think it was anything wrong with the things that I received and the attention I received. Even though it marked me for ministry it also made me tuff, tuff enough not to back down from opposition.

There were times when I even felt like David when he came to bring food to his brothers when Goliath and the Philistines came to destroy the children of Israel 1 Samuel 17:28-29.

Once I was marked for ministry, it seemed like I was always getting in trouble with my siblings and making them mad, but I didn't think I was doing anything wrong I was just being me. Have you ever got in trouble for just being yourself? I had to find out that wasn't my problem, it was the person's problem that didn't like me.

This, which was happening in my life, was training for me. I did not know it, but God was training me to stand up against those that were larger and taller than me. All my life I have been a small person. When I was born I weighed 5 pounds, I was the smallest in my family and even today this is true.

God knew what He had created me to be and do. God knew that demons and the devil were going to come after me to try and defeat me, but what they didn't know was I had been in training and marked for ministry.

Because of my size I had to learn to hold my own, but after I got saved I found out that God was holding me and shielding me from my enemies. I can remember in my adolescence and youth day's people would say things to me and I would literally have a bold comeback. My mother would tell me to be quiet because she thought something bad was about to happen to me, but I wasn't afraid.

I had to also learn that everybody is not like me. Everybody has their own characteristics. As for me I'm a very positive, uplifting, faith walker, strong willed and bold person. This is who I am and always have been. These are my marks for ministry. I need them to be able to handle what this world throws at me.

When I look at the definition of my name it means "the break of day" and truly I'm the definition of my name. This to marked me for ministry because most of my family couldn't understand why I was always cheerful and because of it people drew to me and not them and this caused a discomfort between us. I can come in a room at any time of the day and be cheerful. When the breaking of a new day begins it is just that, a new beginning. Every single day is a new beginning. When a new day comes it brings new opportunities, a new start and a new way of looking at things. In the Bible when children were named it was defining who they were. So, future parents seek God about what to name your children.

You know truly I just believe that God's children's person- alities should be a break of day in all situations. I know some people don't agree with me, but I believe this is the way God wants it to be. When Jesus walked this earth He didn't walk around with His head down, a frown on His face, saying He's not a morning person, don't talk to me until I've had my coffee. No, Jesus was the break of day, the new beginning and the sunshine. Because of me embracing who I am this too became a mark for ministry because in ministry you have to have a high self-esteem; you have to know who you are and whom you belong to. No matter what others say or think about you, you need to know you!

When I look back over my life growing up in my family the only thing that I would want to change is my father's death. I will never know how it would have been if he was still alive - I could only imagine. God knew what He was doing and I have come to accept my father's death was a major role in me being marked for ministry.

If my father wouldn't died I would not be able to relate to others that have loss a parent. This is a mark for ministry because God planned this path for me to help some of you. My father died a hero. The reason why I said that is even though he fell asleep smoking a cigarette and the house caught on fire he got out alive. However, a neighbor thought my siblings and I were still in the house and my father went back in to save us. From the smoke my father was disorientated and he forgot that we were at my grandmother's house with our mother. When the fire department came they found him at the door and he died from smoke inhalation. What a hero!!!

Most of my life I held on to the void because I didn't want to let go of my father. Even though it hurt and it hurt really bad, but at the same time it was a invisible security blanket for me. I could go in my mind and just think about my father and what he meant to me and I had an assurance that there was someone who loved me for me.

I would role play in my mind how it would be if my father was alive to take me to my first day of school, us just hanging out together, me graduating from high school and just having him there when I needed him the most.

You know a mother and father has a very important role

in their children's life. God gave us a task and a how to manual. The how to manual is the Holy Bible. I challenge every parent, every parent to be, every grandparent, every uncle and aunt to search the scriptures and find something to deposit in God's little ones.

As I became older a particular tragedy happened in my life and one of my aunts invited me to a prayer meeting and at the prayer meeting God used my aunt to tell me I have to let go of my father. I obeyed God and instantly I was healed from all the hurt, pain, emptiness and loneliness. I remember that night I had a peaceful night sleep.

What was a mark in my life became ministry. I encourage those of you who may have something similar to my story or maybe it's something else to seek God because He cares for you. God wants to turn your mark into ministry. In Romans 8:28 it says, "And we know all things work together for our good to those who love God, to those who are the called according to His purpose." Because I love Him this mark has worked together with other things for my good.

Now I can think about my father and not feel what I used to feel. It has been 25 years since God took away what I didn't want to let go. Praise be unto God!!!

So how did I make it this far in life with this mark? Truly by the grace and mercies of God and by His wisdom and understanding. God literally told me what I needed to do and not do. God will talk to you directly if you are willing to hear what His plan is for your life. I give Him all the praises and glory for being there for me.

I pray that you would allow the Holy Spirit to minister to you peace, comfort, joy and healing to overcome all that you have been through. Take a moment now to talk to God about the things in your life that you need to be delivered and healed from and expect the Holy Ghost to do what you need done.

Chapter 4

Marriage

Marriage is a union joined between male and female in holy matrimony in the eyes of God.

Marriage is one of the very important decisions that a person can make in their life. When you are considering becoming joined to a person for the rest of your life, you should be **absolutely** sure that you are ready for your life to be changed.

When you say "I do" at the altar it doesn't mean I'm going to still live the single life, I'm not going to submit to my husband, I'm not going to love my wife as Christ loves the Church, I'm not sharing my money, I'm still hanging out with my partners more than my spouse and the list goes on. "I do," means just what it has agreed to. There are no conditions. Either you do or you don't, if you don't, then you shouldn't say, "I do."

When you're considering marriage you also have to be ready to take the "I" out of the marriage. In a marriage there isn't any room for "I". When you become married "I" becomes we and us. This simply means that I am ready to let God prepare me for what He wants to do in my life and through my life in my marriage.

There are some people that want to get married for so many wrong reasons. There are some who get married for companionship, for sex, for someone to help with their bills, out of infatuation, to prove something to someone else, because they want a baby, or because they are getting old. All of these are the wrong reasons to get married and there are so many more wrong reasons.

You have to be absolutely sure that God's will is for you to be married. There are people that were never married, some by choice and others by God's will.

This is the reason that you need to know God's will for your life. If God says His will is for you not to be married, then stop looking to be married. If you go against God's will for your life, you will be miserable and you will continue to have unnecessary troubles and a whole lot of grief.

Paul says, "for I wish that all men were even as I myself. But each one has his own gift from God, one in this manner and another in that." First Corinthians 7:7. God had gifted Paul with not having a desire for marriage. Paul knew that to be able to give his full attention to God and the things of God was far greater than being with any woman and having sex.

If God has gifted you as He gifted Paul in this area, accept it and go through your destiny. Do whatever God tells you to do and kill your flesh. Your life will be so much better.

I believe that if we know God's will for our life and we trust Him to finish it, we would be better off in every area of our life.

I am married to a man that is in prison and he has been in prison our entire marriage. Yes I married him in prison not knowing that by marrying someone that was in prison was going to be a mark for ministry for me.

When I met my husband Fred he was at his lowest, strung out on drugs and no direction in his life. I was an alcoholic, but not admitting to it and if you looked at me you wouldn't known it because I always kept my appearance up. There were times when my husband did look strung out, but wouldn't admit it.

Before my husband went to prison God told me he has potential. What kind of potential I didn't know, all I knew was he had potential for something. After my husband was in prison for a few years his vocabulary and demeanor began to change. My husband began to speak with such eloquence and then I remembered what God had told me about my husband's potential.

When I decided to marry my husband and then go through it my life changed drastically. I decided to get married and I had no one that I could talk to, to help me be a wife and not only a wife, but also a wife that was married to someone in prison serving a life sentence.

Some of my family and others that I knew were against me marrying someone that was sentenced to life in prison. All I knew was I believed I was doing the right thing. I had no idea that God placed me in a marriage that would give Him glory until I kept seeing God's hand in it.

As my life began to change I was struggling with getting rid of the single lifestyle, "I." I just couldn't see myself giving up my comfort zone to become a wife - so "I" didn't. What I did do was take care of my son, focus on him and his education, become faithful to my Church and learn more about God. The more I knew about having a relationship with God the less I wanted a man in my life. I was content with Jesus and me.

During this time God delivered me from things that I didn't know were in me and He was building a foundation for me, a safety nest.

Whatever we go through in life it is for God's purpose and

glory. One of God's purposes for me is to be married to a man in prison until God releases him. Even though some of my family members and others don't agree with it or even understand it, I'm okay with it because its God's will for my life. This is truly a faith walk. God's Word tells us that it's impossible to please Him without faith. Hebrews 11:6. I aim to please God and not man. This faith walk is constantly marking me for ministry.

Through this marriage lifestyle I have learned to put God in His rightful place, my husband in his rightful place, my children in their rightful place and everybody else in their rightful place. I have a balance in my personal life. God wants this for all of us to have a balanced personal life. We can balance our work, friendships, but for some reason our personal life suffers.

Living this type of marriage I don't encourage people to get divorces like I used to do when I was single. When I was single I would tell people you don't have to take that and you don't have to stay with the person, just leave them and get a divorce.

By living this type of marriage I found out my past advice (when I was single) to tell people to get a divorce was really saying quit and give up. Yes, there were many times I wished I wasn't married, but divorce was and is out of the question because I know what God's Word says about divorce.

Living this type of marriage, instead of me telling people that are having problems in their marriage to leave and divorce their spouse I'm saying diligently seek the Lord about it. Spend some time with your spouse and talk about your problems. I also say take off the feelings that you have for your spouse the good and bad feelings and set them aside so you can hear what the Holy Spirit is saying to you. A lot of times we are letting our feelings make decisions that God has not approved of.

There are too many Christian marriages ending in divorce over elementary things. We are allowing this society to tell us what a marriage is and is not. We aren't looking in God's Word anymore to find out our answers. We are getting divorces that aren't approved by God and then getting remarried.

How is it that we Christians can say we believe God's Word, but we don't believe His Word concerning our marriages? In some cases we don't believe that the Holy Ghost can keep us from cheating on our spouse, abusing our spouse and in some cases we won't let the Holy Ghost in our marriage to make it successful.

This mark of marriage that is on my life is there to help my brothers and sisters that want to give up on their marriage. Now my husband is in prison with a life sentence and we are doing all we can to stay married. There have been times when a year would go by and we haven't seen each other and all we had by means of communication was phone calls and letters and God kept the marriage together. Yes we have had our share of problems, test and trials, but we took our hands off and gave it to God to fix it and He did. There are troubled marriages out there and their spouse isn't in prison and they won't invest in their marriage because of unforgiveness and taking the easy way out. This is not the time to be doing your own thing because God is still on the throne and He's still in the judging business.

What I would do when my husband and I were having problems I would go to God and point the finger at my husband. One reason why I would do it was because I felt that I had given up my life for him since he was in prison and he needed to understand and accept my actions.

I had to learn to come to God and to tell Him both sides of the story and not just my husband's faults in my eyes. I had to remember that it takes two to tango. I had to listen to the Holy Ghost when He would tell me something about me that wasn't right. Now I'm not saying that I have it altogether, but it's a whole lot better than it used to be.

I had to learn that marriage was a life long commitment. I had to come to know that marriage is doing time. In other words it's investing time in yourself and your spouse to make it work. The way you do this is by always communicating with one another even when you don't want to. My husband has always been the type of person that when we would have an argument that he didn't want us to end our visit or telephone conversation upset with one another. He would say, " We can't let the sun go down on our wrath." Truly there were some times that I would let the sun go down on our wrath, but not no more.

I was the type of person that didn't want to make up so quickly. I would make my husband suffer by not speaking to him. I also knew that I had the upper hand early in our marriage because my husband couldn't stand it when I wasn't talking to him. I used this in our marriage quite often until I finally came to the reality that what I was doing was wrong.

I had to learn to be quick to hear and slow to speak and slow to wrath because these things did not produce the right-eousness of God. One thing that I knew, and that was from the first time we met we could communicate with each other. When I allowed my flesh to take over then I wasn't communicating with my husband in the way that was pleasing to God.

Another wake up call for me was people were watching me because of the fact that I was married to someone in prison. I didn't realize it, because I was being faithful to my husband by not getting involved with anyone and not divorcing him this caused people to look at me in another way. God had brought attention to me and married people started asking me questions about being married to someone in prison and not just in prison, but serving a life sentence. I had to be honest with them by telling them that it's not me, but God in me.

I believe that God has given everyone a purpose in life whether we fulfill it or not. I know that one part of my purpose is to be married to someone in prison. What a mark for ministry.

Being married I had to look at why so many Christian marriages are in trouble. There were times when my marriage was in trouble, but my husband and I made a decision that no matter how bad it gets not to divorce.

Now this is my opinion and not statistics, I believe some Christians are not being "endurers" in their marriages. I know some people aren't going to like this statement and will probably say, you don't know me and you don't know my story. This is correct. However, once again this is me and not statistics, I believe Christians are marrying people that God never told them to marry. Some Christians are marrying God's choice for their life too soon. We are to wait for God to set the date. One thing is for sure and that is God knows when the time is right to join you in holy matrimony.

In a holy matrimony the two become one flesh, which means that they are stronger now because they are whole ~ they are complete. The devil doesn't want us to become strong. The devil knows that one can chase 1,000 and two can put 10,000 to flight. We need to know that the devil is after our unity because in our unity there is strength. This mark of ministry is strength and it has caused me to endure the problems, test and trials. This mark has caused me to be a positive role model for marriages.

Another thing the devil is after is to cause Christians to divorce without God's permission. In God's Word He is perfectly clear about marriage and divorce. Don't allow the devil to trick you in getting a divorce if God didn't give you permission. Divorce is the last resort not the first choice and in some cases it's not an option.

For those that are married and maybe your marriage is fine right now, ask God to help you to finish on top. For those that are married and your marriage isn't fine right now, ask God what is His will concerning your marriage. Ask God what needs to happen to bring it where God wants it to be.

Another thing that I want to share is if at all possible don't share with someone other than your spouse about your marriage. I don't ever share with anyone about my troubles in my marriage **I am really serious.** I believe that God has all the answers that I need, **so I go to Him.** When people find out it is after the fact and I share when God says so and it has victory attached to it. This mark of ministry will help others.

I say to those that are looking to get married please make sure it is God's will for your life. If it's God's will for your life, make sure you are ready to do the time and to always keep the communication open. Another thing women, if a man comes to you and says he's your husband and it doesn't agree in your spirit don't be afraid to tell him you are not interested in him. You will save yourself a lot of grief from dating when you shouldn't. Men, if a woman comes to you and says God told her she was your wife, then you know she's out of order because the man finds the wife and not the other way around according to Proverbs 18:22.

If anyone that is reading this book is seeing someone in prison and you are considering marrying them, make sure you have really heard from God. If you know of someone that is seeing someone in prison and they are considering marrying that person in prison, please get them a copy of this book. I also want to say I'm not just talking to the female readers concerning this.

I have found out being in this type of marriage that you have to be anointed to live this type of lifestyle. Everybody can't make the sacrifices that this type of marriage calls for.

Now depending on what state you live in, you might not be able to have sex with your spouse. This being the case for my husband and me, but we have found that sex doesn't play the biggest role in the marriage communication and commitment does.

There are married people that know my husband is in prison and they are encouraged by my commitment to first of all God and then to my husband and they say if you can stay married under these conditions so can I. When God told me in First Timothy 4:12 "let no one despise your youth, but be an example to the believers in word, in conduct, in love, in spirit, in faith, in purity." He meant it and I try my very best to obey Him.

This marriage mark of ministry is giving God glory and bearing fruit and for this I praise Him!

Chapter 5

God's Mark

When I think about God's mark I think about Jacob in particular. However, Jacob is not the only person God marked in the Bible. Not only did God mark other people in the Bible He also marked people that are not recorded in the Bible people like me and you. Yes we are marked by God to fulfill a purpose that He has put in all of us. There are some of us who aren't even aware they are marked. Then there are some who know they have been marked by God to live out the destiny that is within them.

When God marked us He didn't do it with a hidden agenda, but to have His will carried out for His glory. I believe that when we recognize the mark on our life and accept it the better off we will be. No this doesn't mean that we are exempted from trouble, pains, disappointments, rejections, being used, being abused, lied on, cheated out of some stuff and the list goes on, but on the contrary these things will happen to us. Even though these things come in our life doesn't mean they will defeat us. For in Romans 8:37 it says, "Yet in all things we are more than conquerors through Him Who loves us."

When you think about being marked by God this is something that we should be proud of and to wear it well. When we really grab a hold of being marked by God we will realize it is an honor and a privilege that God would choose us to be apart of His perfect will. When you think about being marked by God you can say out of the entire world I'm one of the chosen ones.

When God marked us He hand picked us. It's like when you go to the grocery store and you go to the produce department to get some tomatoes you look at all the tomatoes that are before you. As you are looking at these tomatoes there is one that catches your eye. You then go to reach for it to pick it up to find out if it is firm like you like it or soft like you like it. Now if what you saw didn't match what you picked up you put it down and start the process all over. When you handpick the right one you take it home, clean it and then cut it. On the inside of that tomato is just what you expected it to be and it tasted just as you expected it would.

Just like handpicking the right tomato God knew that when He handpicked us what was on the inside of us because He put those things in us and then He put His mark on us. We have to come to the place that we know what's on the inside of us.

Let's look at Jacob's visible mark that resulted from him wrestling with God in Genesis 32:24~25. Prior to these scriptures Jacob was returning to the land of his fathers and his kindred after leaving his Uncle Laban's house as instructed by the LORD Genesis 31:3. In order for Jacob to return to his fathers and kindred land he had to go through the land Seir the country Edom where his brother Esau lived. Since Jacob had not forgotten what he did to his brother he sent messagers to Esau to tell him where he's been, what he has acquired and to find favor in his sight. The report that came back to Jacob caused Jacob to be greatly afraid and distressed. Jacob was so afraid of Esau that he divided his people, flocks, herds and camels into two companies. Genesis 32:3-7

Not only was Jacob afraid of Esau, but his fear caused him to pray to God and bring Him in remembrance of what He said to Abraham and Isaac. Genesis 32:9-12

Jacob gave his servants instructions to go before him and what to give and say to Esau when they met him. After Jacob did that he took his two wives, two maidservants and his eleven sons and crossed over the ford of Jabbok. Then he took them and sent them over the brook and all he had and then he was left alone.

The wrestle begins. In Genesis 32:24-28 it tells us that a Man wrestled with Jacob until the breaking of day (who we know to be God) and Jacob was prevailing until the Man touched Jacob's hip and caused his socket to be out of joint. The Man wanted Jacob to let him go, but Jacob said, "I will not let You go unless You bless me!" After this God changes Jacob's name to Israel and tells him he has struggled with God and man and have prevailed.

In Genesis 32:31 it tells us that Jacob limped on his hip. Jacob's limp was more spiritual then physical. It was all about God's promise to Abraham, Isaac and Jacob's relationship with God and our destiny. When you're marked by God it is noticeable to others, but sometimes we deny it and try to run from it. You can't run from it because it's in you. You cannot take away what God has put in you.

When God touched the socket of Jacob's hip that represented God is in control and when He marks us there's no mistake about it. We all are marked for ministry, we may not have the physical limp like Jacob, but when you search yourself you will discover your mark. God marked Jacob with a limp to remind him who He is, what He promised Abraham, Isaac, him and our future.

Also the mark represented that not only was Jacob victorious, but so are we. God instilled some truths to Israel that he was to pass down to the next generations all the way to us and we are suppose to keep it going.

We as God's children, have to come to our rightful place of who we are and Who we belong to. We are of a royal priesthood whose kingdom is not from this world.

The marks that God has given us are all good because they're for His glory and for the building of His kingdom. We really need to embrace our marks and be proud that the Sovereign God chose us.

I believe God really does care about each and every one of us. I believe He really cares about everything that concerns us.

I encourage you to trust God with every mark in your life. I encourage you to seek after God about your marks, so He can identify them for you and get His wisdom concerning them. I pray that what you have read in this book has helped you, I can't stress it enough don't leave God, stick with Him, He is the only one that sees your whole life and can manage it.

Remember you want your marks to help someone and not hurt them!

Mack Success Group

Mack Success Group

The 6 Timeless Attributes of Success

James Mack
1726 Hamlet Dr.
Ypsilanti, MI 48198
United States

phone 734-483-5226

msg5336@sbcglobal.net
www.authorsden.com/jamesmack

To Order, Call 1-800-AUTHORS, or visit www.iUniverse.com

4UGRAPHICS

TASHA MARIE MURRAY
OWNER/DESIGNER
PHONE:
616.481.5058
EMAIL:
TASHA@4UGRAPHICS.NET

GRAPHICS DESIGN

PRINTING

DESKTOP PUBLISHING

CONSULTING

We make U look good on paper ₅

www.ingramcontent.com/pod-product-compliance
Lightning Source LLC
Chambersburg PA
CBHW060555100426
42742CB00013B/2574